SUPER COOL CONSTRUCTION ACTIVITIES

with MAX AXIOM

by Tammy Enz

Consultant:
Morgan Hynes, Ph.D.
Assistant Professor, Engineering Education
Purdue University
West Lafayette, Indiana

Graphic Library is published by Capstone Press,
710 Roe Crest Drive, North Mankato, Minnesota 56003
www.capstonepub.com

Library of Congress Cataloging-in-Publication Data
Enz, Tammy.
  Super cool construction activities with Max Axiom / by Tammy Enz.
      pages cm.—(Graphic library. Max Axiom science and engineering
activities)
  Audience: Ages 8-14.
  Audience: Grade 4 to 6.
  Summary: "Super Scientist, Max Axiom, presents step-by-step photo-
Illustrated instructions for building a variety of structures and contraptions"—
Provided by publisher.
  Includes bibliographical references and index.
  ISBN 978-1-4914-2078-2 (library binding)
  ISBN 978-1-4914-2282-3 (paperback)
  ISBN 978-1-4914-2296-0 (eBook PDF)
  1. Structural engineering—Juvenile literature. 2. Building—Juvenile literature.
3. Structural engineering—Comic books, strips, etc. 4. Building—Comic books,
strips, etc. 5. Graphic novels. I. Title.
  TA634.E593 2015
  624—dc23   2014027883

Editor
Christopher L. Harbo

Art Director
Nathan Gassman

Designer
Tracy McCabe

Production Specialist
Katy LaVigne

Cover Illustration
Marcelo Baez

Project Creation
Sarah Schuette and Marcy Morin

Photographs by Capstone Studio:
Karon Dubke

Printed in the United States of
America in Stevens Point,
Wisconsin.
092014   008479WZS15

Table of Contents

Welcome to my lab! You're just in time to see my newest construction project.

I built these three models to test different materials used in levees to protect cities.

CLAY

SOIL

ROCK

As you can see, this levee is built of rock. The other two are constructed with soil and clay.

By adding some water, we'll see which one works the best.

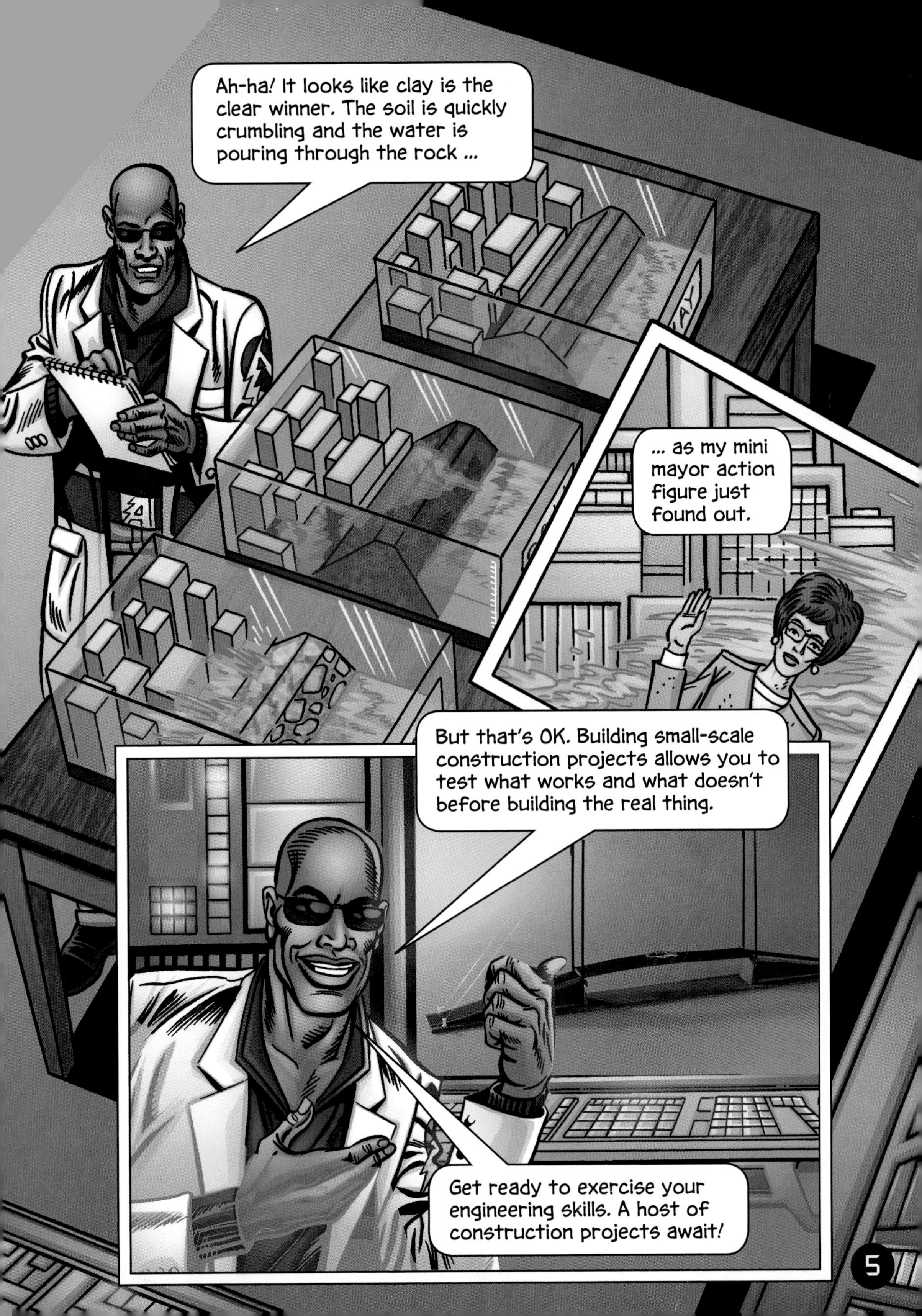
Ah-ha! It looks like clay is the clear winner. The soil is quickly crumbling and the water is pouring through the rock ...
... as my mini mayor action figure just found out.
But that's OK. Building small-scale construction projects allows you to test what works and what doesn't before building the real thing.
Get ready to exercise your engineering skills. A host of construction projects await!

LEVEE

It's your turn to build a levee. These large structures are built in a river's **floodplain** to protect homes and cities. Engineers often combine different materials to improve a levee's strength. Construct your own levee design with a few simple supplies.

YOU'LL NEED

egg carton

scissors

large container with a smooth bottom

gravel

sand

water

pottery clay

rolling pin

1. Using the scissors, cut off four or five egg cups from the egg carton. Place these upside down on one side of the large container. They represent buildings in a floodplain.

2. Create a wall of gravel 2 to 3 inches (5 to 7 centimeters) high down the center of the container.

3. Mix a small amount of water with the sand to make it damp. Pack sand around the gravel wall.

4. Roll and pat the clay into a flat sheet long enough and wide enough to cover the levee. Place the sheet over the levee. Smooth it and press its edges to the sides and bottom of the container to form a tight seal.

5. Slowly fill the side of the container opposite the egg cups with water to represent rising floodwaters.

6. Note areas where the wall is weak or leaky. Apply more gravel to make parts of the wall stronger. Add clay to fill in leaks.

⚡ AXIOM ALTERNATIVE

Engineers use fabrics called geotextiles to prevent soil from washing away during floods. Try wrapping your levee with pieces of a mesh fruit bag to act like geo-fabric. Does the fruit bag strengthen the levee?

floodplain—an area of low land near a stream or river that becomes flooded during heavy rains

Ancient builders often built stone arches without using any cement. How did they do this? The secret is the keystone at the very top of an arch. This wedge-shaped stone holds all the pieces together. Test out the keystone concept with a simple foam arch.

YOU'LL NEED

18-inch (46-cm) square of 2-inch- (5-cm-) thick foam

electric foam cutter

ruler

pencil

SAFETY FIRST

Ask an adult for permission to use an electric foam cutter before starting this project.

PLAN OF ACTION

1. Cut a 5-inch (13-cm) square from the foam.

2. Measure and mark a spot 1½ inches (4 cm) in from one corner of the square. Draw a line from this mark to the opposite corner of the square. Cut along the line to make a truncated triangle.

3. Repeat steps 1 and 2 to make a second identical shape.

4. Draw a trapezoid on the remaining foam. Make it 2 inches (5 cm) along the base, 1½ inches (4 cm) along its top, and 1 inch (2.5 cm) high. Cut out this shape.

5. Repeat step 4 four more times to make additional trapezoids with the same dimensions.

6. Set the truncated triangles upright so they sit about 4½ inches (11 cm) apart. These triangles will be the supports for the arch.

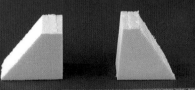

7. Begin stacking the slanted edges of the trapezoids onto the supports to begin forming an arch shape. Stack two on each support, holding them in place as you stack.

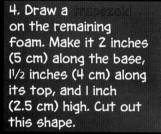

8. Have a friend place the final trapezoid, the "keystone," between the stacks to finish the arch and lock the blocks into place.

⚡ AXIOM ALTERNATIVE

Make additional foam blocks and build a bridge or a span of connected arches. Try doubling or tripling the dimensions of your foam blocks to make larger arches and structures. How tall can you make your arch?

truncate—to shorten by cutting off the top of an object

trapezoid—a shape with four sides of which only two are parallel

FREEWAY RAMP

A busy city freeway overpass is a web of roads and ramps twisting and weaving around and through each other. Transportation engineers design circular ramps so drivers can safely enter and exit freeways. These ramps must allow cars to make tight turns without crashing or spinning off the road. Test out your engineering skills by building a freeway ramp to keep a marble on a safe course.

YOU'LL NEED

2 30-inch- (76-cm-) long giftwrap tubes

ruler

sharpened pencil

11 unsharpened pencils

2 12-inch- (30-cm-) long paper towel tubes

hot glue gun

12 sturdy paper plates

scissors

packing tape

marble

SAFETY FIRST

Ask an adult for permission to use a hot glue gun before starting this project.

1. Measure and mark I inch (2.5 cm), 9 inches (23 cm), 17 inches (43 cm), 23 inches (58 cm), and 29 inches (73 cm) from one end of a giftwrap tube. Use a sharpened pencil to poke a hole at each of these marks. Repeat this step with the other giftwrap tube.

2. Insert unsharpened pencils into the holes made in step I to connect the tubes.

3. Mark I inch (2.5 cm) from each end of both paper towel tubes. Connect them together as in step 2.

4. Lay the smaller rectangle flat on the floor. Poke holes on the top faces of the tubes, 90 degrees from the first holes. These holes will be perpendicular to the pencils holding the rectangle together. Insert an unsharpened pencil into each of these holes.

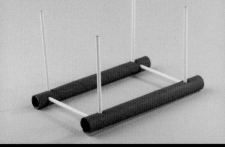

5. Stand the small and large rectangles next to each other. Mark spots where the pencils in the small rectangle touch the large rectangle. Punch holes at these locations and insert the unsharpened pencil ends to make a tower.

perpendicular—describes two lines that intersect at a 90-degree angle; two lines that form the letter T are perpendicular to each other

6. Adjust the pencils and tubes to make the tower square. Use hot glue to secure the pencils in place.

7. Cut the outside rims from the paper plates. Leave only ½ inch (1 cm) of the flat center part of the plate. Cut away the rest of the plate and discard.

8. Turn one rim upside down and lay it on top of another rim to form a trough. Tape the rims to each other on their undersides. Continue taping rims together to form a long trough coil.

9. Tape one end of the coil to the highest pencil on the tower. Begin winding it around one of the giftwrap uprights. Test each curve by rolling a marble on it to make sure the marble can travel along the curve without flying off. Tape the coil to the upright as you move your way down the structure, constantly testing your roadway.

10. When the trough reaches the ground, test the entire structure by rolling a marble from top to bottom. Adjust the trough as needed so the marble follows it all the way down.

AXIOM ALTERNATIVE

Construct another spiraling roadway. Attach it to the other giftwrap upright and connect the roadways. Then race marbles on each of the roadways, trying not to crash them.

trough—a long, narrow channel

SUSPENSION BRIDGE

Suspension bridges use anchored cables to carry the weight of their bridge decks. They are famous for spanning larger gaps than other types of bridges. They easily span distances from 2,000 to 7,000 feet (600 to 2,100 meters). Prepare to experience the awesome engineering behind the suspension bridge.

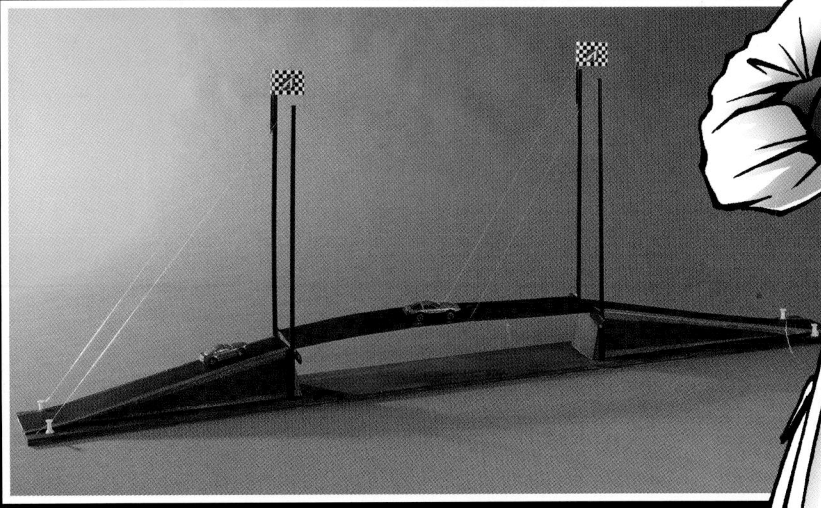

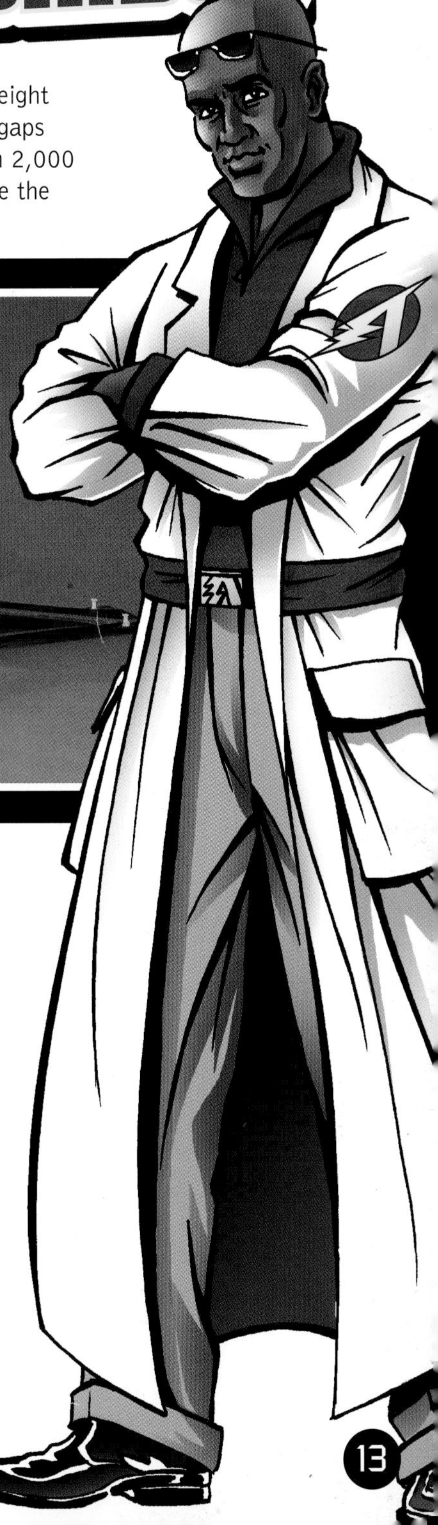

YOU'LL NEED

- 34-inch x 4¼-inch (86-cm x 11-cm) piece of plywood
- ruler
- pencil
- drill
- 3/16-inch (5-mm) drill bit
- 4 wooden skewers
- utility knife
- hot glue gun
- 2 wooden craft sticks
- 12½-inch x 3-inch (32-cm x 8-cm) piece of paper
- tape
- 4 pushpins
- 2 60-inch- (152-cm-) long pieces of fishing line
- empty cardboard cereal box
- scissors

continued

1. Measure and draw lines ½ inch (1 cm) in from each of the plywood's long edges. Measuring from a short edge of the plywood, make marks at 1 inch (2.5 cm), 11 inches (28 cm), 23 inches (58 cm), and 33 inches (84 cm) on both lines. Ask an adult to drill holes at each of these marks.

2. With an adult's help, use the utility knife to slice a ½-inch (1-cm) slit into the blunt ends of each of the skewers.

3. Insert the pointed end of each skewer into each of the four center-most holes in the plywood. Rotate the skewers so the slits are parallel to the long sides of the plywood. Secure the skewers in place with hot glue.

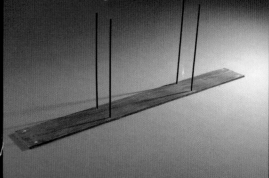

4. Measure and mark 2 inches (5 cm) up from the bottom of each upright skewer. Place the top edge of a craft stick across each set of skewers at this mark. Glue the craft sticks in place to make two H shapes.

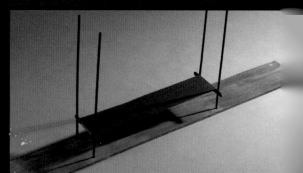

5. Measure and mark a line ¼ inch (0.5 cm) from each short end of the paper strip. Fold the paper at these marks and unfold halfway. Hang the folded edges over the craft sticks. Tape the edges to the craft sticks to make the bridge deck.

6. Firmly push a pin into each of the remaining holes on the piece of plywood.

7. Wrap and tie one end of a piece of fishing line around one of the pushpins. Thread it up through the slit on the nearest upright and under the center of the paper deck.

8. Tape the line to the underside of the paper and then continue threading it through the slit in the adjoining upright. Wrap and tie the end of the line around the adjacent pushpin. Make sure the fishing line is pulled taut but the deck remains flat.

9. Repeat steps 7 and 8 at the opposite end of the bridge.

10. Lay the cereal box flat. Measure and mark 2 inches (5 cm) from one corner along the bottom of the box. Measure and mark 10 inches (25.5 cm) from this corner along the side of the box. Draw a straight line between these points. Flip the box and repeat. Cut along these lines to form a wedge.

11. Repeat step 10 with the other bottom corner of the box. Place the wedges at either end of the bridge to form ramped abutments.

12. Place a small vehicle on the bridge to see the suspension cables tighten to hold its weight.

AXIOM ALTERNATIVE

Experiment with different bridge deck materials. Can you get a cellophane bridge deck to work? Does a cardboard deck make a stronger bridge?

WASTEWATER TREATMENT PLANT

Ever wonder what happens to wastewater when you flush the toilet or drain a sink? Construct a simple two-tank **septic system** to separate solids and to clean liquids before returning water to the environment.

YOU'LL NEED

2-liter soda bottle

ruler

marker

utility knife

milk jug

14-inch x 8-inch (36-cm x 20-cm) piece of plywood

2 drink straws

hot glue gun

10-inch- (25-cm-) long 2 x 4 board

2 cotton balls

clean sand

clean gravel

small dish

muddy water

SAFETY FIRST

Ask an adult for permission to use a utility knife and hot glue gun before starting this project.

septic system—a drainage system with a tank used to treat wastewater

1. Draw an oval that is about 2 inches (5 cm) wide by 5 inches (13 cm) long on the 2-liter bottle. The oval should start at the bottom of one of the bottle's feet. Carefully cut the oval out with the utility knife.

2. Lay the milk jug on its side. Use the utility knife to carefully cut out a large square from its top side.

3. Lay the two straws 2 inches (5 cm) apart on the plywood. One end of each straw should be even with one of the plywood's short sides. Secure the straws in place with hot glue.

4. Lay the 2-liter bottle between the two straws with the oval hole on top. Make its bottom even with the straw ends.

5. Place one end of the 2 x 4 behind the bottom of the 2-liter bottle. Lay the milk jug on the 2 x 4 with its hole facing up. Allow the jug's spout to overlap the 2-liter bottle's oval hole.

7. Pack sand into the front end of the bottle, nearest the cotton balls.

8. Fill the rest of the bottle with gravel.

9. Place the dish under the neck of the bottle.

10. Slowly pour muddy water into the hole of the milk jug.

11. Watch as the solids in the water sink to the bottom of the jug. The rest of the water will begin flowing into the soda bottle to be cleaned by the gravel and sand. It will exit the system as clean water. Continue pouring in muddy water.

Each time its level reaches the level of the spout, it will trickle into the gravel. (Although the exiting water looks clean, do not drink it because the system will not remove all the bacteria and chemicals.)

12. Rinse out the solids in the first tank as it begins to fill up.

AXIOM ALTERNATIVE

In a real-life septic system, solids are pumped out as the tank fills up. Design a system to pump out the solids as they collect in the first tank. A hose with a large syringe for a pump might do the job.

HYDRAULIC DRAWBRIDGE

A traffic bridge crossing a shipping channel can pose big problems for ships that are too large to pass under it. Engineers have designed the perfect compromise—the drawbridge. A drawbridge lifts and lowers to allow ships to pass under it. See how it works with this hydraulic-powered drawbridge.

YOU'LL NEED

3 wooden skewers

ruler

pencil

scissors

4 cardboard toilet paper tubes

sharp nail

8 jumbo wooden craft sticks

hot glue gun

2 small eyelet screws

10½-inch x 5½-inch (27-cm x 14-cm) piece of cardboard

2 syringes

12-inch- (30-cm-) long plastic hose with an 1/8-inch (3-mm) inside diameter

SAFETY FIRST

Ask an adult for permission to use a hot glue gun before starting this project.

continued

PLAN OF ACTION

1. Measure and mark 4½ inches (11 cm) from the blunt end of each of the skewers. Clip off this section with a scissors and discard the rest of the skewer.

2. Measure and mark ½ inch (1 cm) from one end of two cardboard tubes. Poke holes through these marks with the sharp nail. Insert a skewer into the hole in one of the tubes. Stick the other end of the skewer into the hole in the other tube.

3. Measure and make two marks on each of the remaining tubes. Make them ½ inch (1 cm) from one of the ends and ½ inch (1 cm) apart. Punch poles at these marks and connect the tubes with two parallel skewers.

4. Trim one rounded end from six of the craft sticks with a scissors.

5. Lay three sticks from step 4 side-by-side with their square ends even. Repeat with the three remaining sticks. Bring the square ends together.

6. Measure and cut 2-inch (5-cm) sections from the remaining sticks. Lay one 2-inch (5-cm) segment across the joint between the sets of sticks. Glue in place. Lay the remaining 2-inch (5-cm) pieces about 1 inch (2.5 cm) from either end of the sticks. Glue in place to finish the bridge deck.

7. Screw the eyelet screws into the center of one of the 2-inch (5-cm) end pieces on the bridge deck. Space the eyelets about 1½ inches (4 cm) apart. Make sure the screws don't pierce the other side of the sticks.

8. Slide out one end of the skewer from the tubes connected in step 2. Thread the eyelets onto the skewer and replace the cardboard tube.

9. Place the whole bridge structure on top of the cardboard piece. Align the tubes in each corner so that their edges are even with the sides of the cardboard. Glue in place.

10. Insert each of the syringe tips into either end of the hose. Remove one of the syringe's plungers. Close the plunger on the other syringe. With a friend's help, fill the empty syringe with water.

Then pull the other syringe's plunger to fill the hose and syringe with water. Place the plunger back into the empty syringe. Adjust the syringes so that as one opens, the other closes.

11. Insert the back end of one syringe between the skewers from step 3. Allow the syringe's flanges to rest on skewers along the center of their span. Glue the flanges in place.

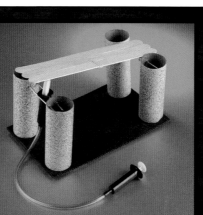

12. Push and pull the other plunger to raise and lower the bridge.

ange—a lip or edge that sticks out from something

[redacted] PYRAMID

When the Egyptians built the pyramids, they picked a shape they knew could stand the test of time. But why have these structures lasted for thousands of years? Aside from their stone construction, a pyramid's wide base and narrow peak is incredibly stable. Test the strength and stability of a pyramid with a structure made only with newspaper and tape.

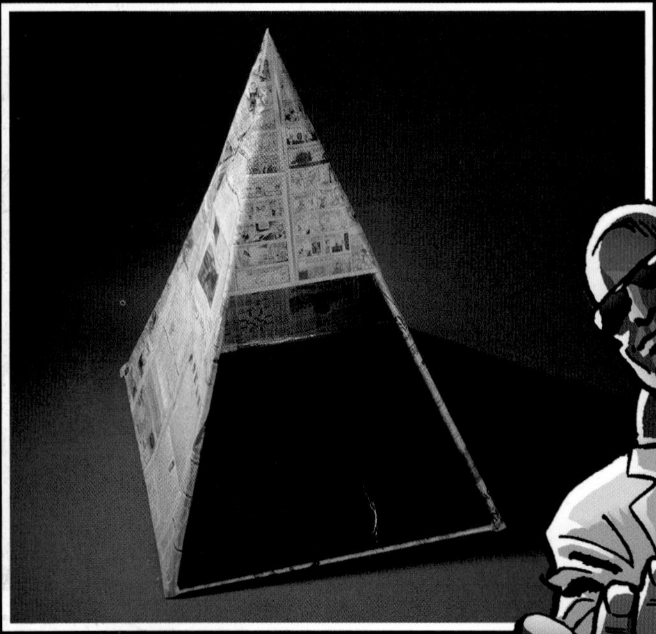

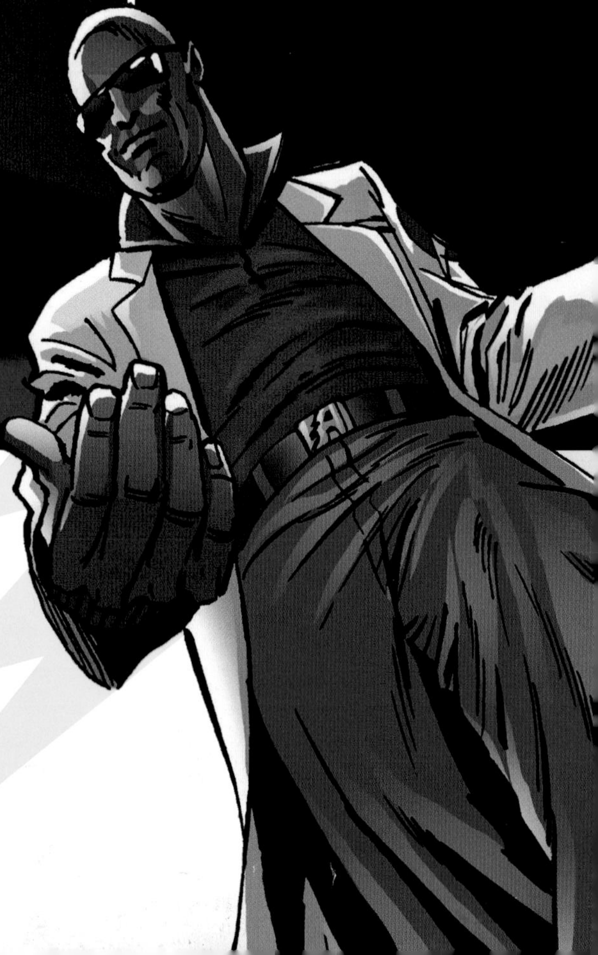

YOU'LL NEED

- newspaper (30 to 40 sheets)
- packing tape
- ruler
- scissors
- stapler
- pencil

1. Lay two sheets of newspaper side-by-side with their short sides touching. Tape the short sides together using long strips of packing tape.

2. Tightly roll the sheets diagonally into a tube. Tape the loose corner to keep the tube rolled.

3. Cut about 5 inches (13 cm) from each end of the tube. Wrap a piece of packing tape around each end to strengthen it.

4. Repeat steps 1 through 3 to make three more tubes. Make them the same length as the first tube.

5. Lay three sheets of newspaper side-by-side with their short sides touching. Tape and roll them into a tube in the same manner outlined in steps 1 and 2. Then cut 5 inches (13 cm) off each end of the tube.

continued

6. Repeat step 5 to create three more tubes. Make each of these tubes the same length as the tube in that step.

tubes in a square shape with their ends overlapping.

8. Staple the ends together to make the base of the pyramid.

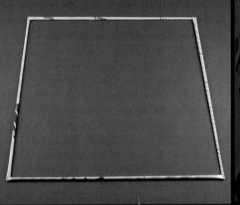

10. Stand up the long tubes and staple their ends together over the center of the square to form the skeleton of the pyramid.

9. Staple one end of each longer tube to one of the base's corners. Make sure the other end of each long tube angles diagonally inward toward the center of the square.

11. Lay several pieces of newspaper side-by-side to form a sheet large enough to cover one side of the pyramid. Tape the papers together.

13. Wrap the newspaper triangle around the tubes and tape it in place.

12. Lay one side of the pyramid on the top of the newspaper sheets. Trace the outline of the triangle about 1 inch (2.5 cm) larger than the triangle on each side. Cut along these lines.

14. Repeat steps 10 through 12 to cover two additional sides of the pyramid.

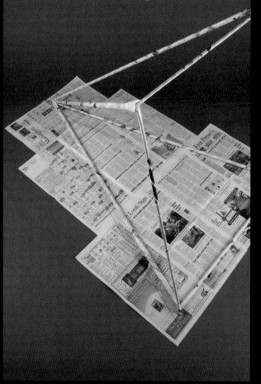

15. Cut a smaller triangle out of a single sheet of newspaper and tape at the top of the remaining side of the pyramid to allow room to crawl into it.

⚡ AXIOM ALTERNATIVE

Compare your pyramid's strength to other newspaper shapes. Try building a cube-shaped fort with the same size base as your pyramid. Which structure is stronger?

LOCK AND DAM

Dams on rivers harness energy to create electricity. They also control water levels to help ships and barges travel safely. But the water levels on opposite sides of a dam often differ by dozens of feet. How do boats safely move from one water level to the other? The answer is a **lock** system. Float your own miniature boat through a lock and dam system to see how it works.

YOU'LL NEED

2 clean 64-fluid-ounce (1.89-liter) juice boxes with screw cap lids

heavy duty shears

ruler

duct tape

foam earplug

PLAN OF ACTION

1. Carefully cut off the glued seam on the top of one of the boxes.

2. Open the box top. Lay it on its side with the spout facing upwards. Carefully cut away the top panel with the spout attached.

3. Repeat steps 1 and 2 with the other box.

4. Lay one box inside the other with their bottoms opposite each other to form a larger rectangular box. Overlap the boxes by about 2 inches (5 cm).

5. Tape the boxes together with strips of duct tape. Tape along the inside overlap and the outside overlap to make the box watertight.

6. Lay one of the pieces of cut away cardboard (with the spout attached) flat. Measure and mark a line parallel to, and 7 inches (18 cm) from, the end nearest the spout. Cut along this line.

lock—an area of water with gates at both ends; locks help ships move from one water level to another

continued

7. Measure and mark another line parallel to, and 4 inches (10 cm) from, the end nearest the spout. Bend the spout forward at this line, creasing it at a 90-degree angle.

8. Stand this piece of cardboard inside the box. Place it 7½ inches (19 cm) from one end of the box. The spout should face away from the 7½-inch (19-cm) section you just created. Tape the cardboard in place along all sides to make it waterproof.

9. Lay the other piece of cardboard (with the spout) flat. Measure and mark a line parallel to, and 4 inches (10 cm) from, the end nearest the spout. Cut along this line.

10. Place this cardboard piece upright inside the box 3 inches (8 cm) from the previous piece. The spout should be near the bottom of the box. It should also face the same direction as the other spout. Tape this cardboard piece in place along all sides.

Cut the foam earplug in half
ngthwise to make a small boat.

12. With the caps on each of the spouts, place
the earplug in the first compartment you
constructed. Fill this compartment to the
top with water. Open the cap to this
compartment. Notice how the water
level becomes equal in the first two
compartments. Gently push the boat
through the spout into the
second compartment.

3. Open the lower cap. Allow the
ater level to equalize with the
ower pool so the boat can move
o the third compartment.

14. To send the boat back upstream, move the boat back
to the middle compartment and close the lower cap. Add
more water to the first compartment to move the boat
back to the higher water level.

15. Adjust the water levels and repeat.

⚡ AXIOM ALTERNATIVE

*A river has continuously flowing water that refills each pool as
each gate opens. Attach a hose and drain to the system to provide a
continuous stream of water to better represent an actual river system.*

Glossary

abutment (a-BUT-muhnt)—the part of a structure that directly receives thrust or pressure

flange (FLANJ)—a lip or edge that sticks out from something

floodplain (FLUHD-playn)—an area of low land near a stream or river that becomes flooded during heavy rains

lock (LOK)—an area of water with gates at both ends; locks help ships move from one water level to another

parallel (PAIR-uh-lel)—side by side at an equal distance between all points

perpendicular (pur-puhn-DIK-yuh-lur)—describes two lines that intersect at a 90-degree angle; two lines that form the letter T are perpendicular to each other

septic system (SEP-tik SISS-tuhm)—a drainage system with a tank used to treat wastewater

trapezoid (TRAP-uh-zoid)—a shape with four sides of which only two are parallel

trough (TRAWF)—a long, narrow channel

truncate (TRUHNGK-ate)—to shorten by cutting off the top of an object

Read More

Brasch, Nicolas. *Amazing Built Structures*. The Technology Behind. Mankato, Minn.: Smart Apple Media, 2011.

Hanson, Anders. *Cool Structures: Creative Activities That Make Math & Science Fun for Kids!* Cool Art with Math & Science. Minneapolis: ABDO Publishing Company, 2014.

Latham, Donna. *Bridges and Tunnels: Investigate Feats of Engineering*. Build It Yourself Series. White River Junction, Vt.: Nomad Press, 2012.

Internet Sites

FactHound offers a safe, fun way to find Internet sites related to this book. All of the sites on FactHound have been researched by our staff.

Here's all you do:

Visit *www.facthound.com*

Type in this code: 9781491420782

Check out projects, games and lots more at
www.capstonekids.com

Index